TOO MANY CRUCIBLES

Matt Lyle

I0139555

BROADWAY PLAY PUBLISHING INC
New York
www.broadwayplaypub.com
info@broadwayplaypub.com

TOO MANY CRUCIBLES
© Copyright 2019 Matt Lyle

Cover art by Kim Lyle

First edition: March 2019
I S B N: 978-0-88145-826-8

Book design: Marie Donovan
Page make-up: Adobe InDesign
Typeface: Palatino

ACKNOWLEDGMENTS

Thanks and love to the following: Kim, Anna, Matt Coleman, Ashley White and all the folks at Imprint Theatreworks, Kevin Moriarty and the Dallas Theater Center, Max Hartman, and Denise Lee.

CHARACTERS & SETTING

Minimum casting—8 actors (4 F, 4 M). Below is the suggested doubling though there may be other permutations.

Actress 1:
VERITY, *a simple farmer who grew up in a conservative household*

Actress 2:
ZWENA, *a slave from Barbados*
SANDY, *a member of a very socially conscious chat group*

Actress 3:
PURITAN WOMAN 1 *and* PURITAN WOMAN 4
MARY, *a young lady*
GOODY BENDING, *the female challenger who lost the election to* DUNNING KRUGER
JUDGE STURM, *the judge at the witch trial*
TESSA, *a member of a very socially conscious chat group*

Actress 4:
PURITAN WOMAN 2 *and* PURITAN WOMAN 3
STANDISH THE GOAT, ZEKE's *goat*
TRINA. *a duplicitous young woman*
FED, *an officer of the law*

Actor 1:
ZEKE, *a simple but liberal minded farmer*
DOTTY, *a young girl*

Actor 2:

DUNNING KRUGER, *the newly elected reverend*
MARVIN, *a member of a very socially conscious chat group*

Actor 3:

DEVIN HARRIS - DUNNING KRUGER'*s chief of staff*
DEFENSE ATTORNEY
REVEREND HALE, *a former "witch finder" who has seen the
    error of his ways*
PURITAN MAN 1 *and* 2
DIRK, *a member of a very socially conscious chat group*
HECKLER, *V O*
JAILER

Actor 4:

DENTIST, ZEKE'*s dentist*
CHEECH, *a lovable brute*
HORNER, DOTTY *and* TRINA'*s father*
PROSECUTOR
PURITAN MAN 3
SATAN

1692 in Peabody, Massachusetts

AUTHOR'S NOTES

TOO MANY CRUCIBLES was born out of my love of bits and my current state of fear and loathing caused by our country's political climate. Basically, I wish we could all be so much more understanding of each other…well, not everyone…some people are certainly worthy of disdain and they catch a heap of it in this play… But everyone else needs to, you know, give everyone else a break already.

In my experience, the jokes and bits in TOO MANY CRUCIBLES (and there are SO many) land best when everyone is fully invested in the super high stakes at play. Much of it carries the same life and death stakes as Miller's much better but way less funny THE CRUCIBLE. When a couple fights, they REALLY fight even though the fight is full of jokes. You get the drift. Have fun.

Also, I don't think having the actor playing Dunning Kruger do a Donald Trump impersonation would work as well as an original character who is equally angry and stupid. I guess I could be wrong about that, but that's my intuition.

ACT ONE

(Lights up on ZEKE, *a simple Puritan farmer, in a prison cell. He's praying urgently.)*

ZEKE: Oh, lord, it's me. Ezekiel. Ezekiel Farmer? Don't know if ye remember me. I haft not prayed lo these many years because I'm—I'm one hundred percent positive you're not up there. Still, I could really use thy help. I'm imprisoned and waiting to be executed. And lord, I know that I'm not as strong of a Christian as my Puritan brethren who love thee above all else whereas I tend to love curling up with a good book and a glass of Merlot in between four naked women above all else… And maybe a couple of guys, I mean, depending on the guys, of course… Heh, kidding, Lord. Kidding… Dear God! I know that I am just a humble farmer and that I stare a little too long whenever I see someone churning butter…and people are ALWAYS churning butter around here. How much butter do people need!? And—and I literally can't think of one commandment right now. Not one! Thou shalt not something something, I don't know! Who cares!? I figure it's the 1600s in Peabody, Massachusetts, pretty much everything fun is considered a mortal sin so just keep doin' watchyou doin' playboy, you know? Heh… sorry. I joke when I'm nervous. I know that I'm not thy perfect child and pretty much an atheist but I could use a miracle oh great heavenly one. They're going to hang me by my neck until I'm dead which is, I understand,

the worst way to be hung. Heh...well, anyway...
Just to catch you up on the situation since I can only
assume you've been napping while the world just
fucking burns... It started last November, on election
night, when against all odds...and good taste, Dunning
Kruger...won.

(Lights up on DUNNING KRUGER *giving a speech)*

DUNNING: Look at this crowd! Look at this crowd!
There's got to be forty, fifty people here. Incredible.
Incredible. They said Dunning Kruger couldn't win but
Dunning Kruger won! And it was a beautiful thing...
And to my honorable opponent, Goody Bending—

CROWD: *(Starts chanting)* Burn her up!

*(*DUNNING *loves it but he halts them.)*

DUNNING: No, we shall not burn her. We shall not...
though she vex us!

(They boo.)

DUNNING: Oh, ho! She vexes us greatly! She vexes us so
greatly. So, so greatly. But it's up to me to be the bigger
man... and ye have to be a pretty big man to be bigger
than Goody Constant Bending!

*(*DUNNING *pantomimes being fat for a few moments and the
crowd loves it and it eggs him on.)*

DUNNING: Ohhh, I'm fat! HA! That woman is ugly!!
And what use is an ugly woman, am I right?!?!?

(They cheer. Beat)

DUNNING: Now, let us pray.

(Lights off of DUNNING *and back on* ZEKE *who is in a
dentist's chair being examined by his* DENTIST.*)*

ZEKE: Actually, it really started before that, about a
year ago when I was at my dentist's office—

DENTIST: Hmmm... Hast thou been praying for the spaces between thy teeth after every meal?

ZEKE: Oh, yeah, I do.

DENTIST: Verily?

ZEKE: Uhh...

DENTIST: I can tell thou hasn't been praying because of thy rampant gum disease.

ZEKE: Really?

DENTIST: They just—see, they just all move around in there if ye—

ZEKE: C'mon—

DENTIST: Look how loose—

ZEKE: Well, stop—

DENTIST: —See—

ZEKE: —Stop wiggling them—

DENTIST: Okay. Jeez.

ZEKE: I'll pray more. I promise.

(The DENTIST gets out a Medievel dental tool.)

DENTIST: I'm afraid this is going to hurt, Brother Farmer.

ZEKE: Okay.

(ZEKE braces for dental pain. Beat)

DENTIST: I've been sleeping with thy wife for a month.

(Beat)

ZEKE: What? What?!

DENTIST: I regret it deeply.

ZEKE: Not as much as I regret it—

(ZEKE's wife, VERITY FARMER enters. He goes to her.)

ZEKE: You've been schtupping the dentist?!

VERITY: You've rolled in the hay with Goody Chaderton.

ZEKE: We were literally rolling in hay. It wasn't a euphemism.

VERITY: That's weird—

ZEKE: That's why I was covered in ticks—

VERITY: —I thought SHE gave you ticks—

ZEKE: Wha?

VERITY: —Serves you right

ZEKE: Wha— No. No. Though I admit I have tried to lay with many women. I keep striking out. The closest I've gotten is sitting with a woman.

VERITY: See! We've grown apart for the better part of a year.

ZEKE: There is a distance.

VERITY: What's the source of the distance?

ZEKE: I have no idea. *(He speaks to us/God.)* I knew. It was the election. It had driven us apart.

VERITY: He's got chutzpah!

ZEKE: Well, one man's chutzpah is another man's severe personality disorder.

VERITY: Thee said thyself men like him have made the new world what it is.

ZEKE: Yes, but I was referring to the New World being a place of disease and genocide—

VERITY: —Okay, now—

ZEKE: And genocide, did I mention genocide?

VERITY: I for one am not convinced there has been any genocide.

ZEKE: What?

VERITY: False flag.

(Beat. Lights down on VERITY*)*

ZEKE: False Flag— You see what I was dealing with, Lord? I'm not a political man by nature. But I knew for the first time, I had an obligation to say what I knew in my heart was true—that Dunning Kruger was an insane, web toed cat fart. And he was about to be elected to the highest office in the land, Reverend of Peabody. And it was tearing our community apart.

(Lights up on a PURITAN *couple. They speak to us, interview style.)*

PURITAN MAN #1: I greatly admire the way he doesn't feel he needs to know anything about the Bible to be the head of God's Holy Church.

*(*PURITAN WOMAN #1 *[his wife] laughs.)*

PURITAN MAN #1: Ha! Right?

*(*PURITAN MAN #1 *looks at* PURITAN WOMAN #1, *confused. Beat)*

PURITAN WOMAN #1: Oh, you're serious?

(Another PURITAN WOMAN *walks past.)*

PURITAN WOMAN #1: He hates women!

PURITAN WOMAN #2: That's great! I hate women, too!

PURITAN WOMAN #1: But you're a woman!

PURITAN WOMAN #2: That's great! I hate women, too!

(Lights down on them and lights up on VERITY *and* ZEKE *reading in bed.)*

ZEKE: Whatchya readin'?

VERITY: Bible. Thee?

ZEKE: Same. Same. *(Pause)* Did thee?

VERITY: Shine thy hat buckle?

ZEKE: Yeah.

VERITY: It's shiny enough to see thy sins in it.

ZEKE: Thanks, honey.

(Pause. ZEKE *tries to kiss* VERITY *and she rebuffs him.)*

ZEKE: I want to have a baby!

VERITY: Now—

ZEKE: —I know—

VERITY: —We've talked about this.

ZEKE: We don't have to make a baby, but let's at least practice. *(He kisses her.)* Tell me I'm sexy.

VERITY: You're sexy—

ZEKE: —You don't like me, you just like my missionary style.

VERITY: Honey

ZEKE: —We can role play. You can be the farmer's wife and I'll be the farmer—

VERITY: —But we are farmers—

ZEKE: —We'll be different farmers.

VERITY: Zeke—

ZEKE: *(As a character.)* —I don't know a Zeke.

VERITY: Zeke, stop!

(Beat)

ZEKE: I love you.

VERITY: I love you, too!

ZEKE: Then get the butter churn out of the closet and let's do this—

VERITY: —No. I—I love you sooooo much.

ZEKE: And I love you sooooo much. *(Beat)* But?

VERITY: I…

ZEKE: I know. Things are not good between us right now.

VERITY: And it's really nobody's fault. It's just that this period of time, what's happening in the world is just highlighting our inherent differences.

ZEKE: Right. I admit we've always been very different people.

VERITY: We just see the world differently. That's all. And that's okay.

ZEKE: That's okay. Absolutely.

VERITY: I grew up with my parents being slaughtered by savages and you grew up on the lower East Side.

ZEKE: *(Aside)* My parents ran a profitable cranberry sauce company.

VERITY: Right. You come from a family with money and I come from a family with rickets.

ZEKE: I went to a liberal arts college and you are profoundly illiterate.

VERITY: I'm the first person in my family not to die from dysentery—

ZEKE: Not yet, anyway—

VERITY: —Not yet. See?! You can't understand where I'm coming from. So, I guess what I'm saying is I'm salt of the earth and you're a total...a total...libtard!!

ZEKE: Libt— Why— Racist!

VERITY: Cuck!

ZEKE: Racist!

VERITY: Snowflake!

ZEKE: Uh— Racist!

VERITY: You represent the intellectual elite!

ZEKE: I don't see how that's not a compliment!

VERITY: Oh, suck off!

ZEKE: You suck off! *(Aside)* Right in the middle of the best conversation we've had in months we start calling each other names and telling each other to suck off. And we used to be so close.

VERITY: *(To us)* Early in our relationship we had a vaudeville act.

ZEKE: One of the all time great Puritan male/female comedy duos.

VERITY: We were the only one.

ZEKE: Right. We were terrible.

VERITY: Which was a good thing since Puritans consider laughter a mortal sin.

(Suddenly VERITY and ZEKE are in a spotlight doing their act.)

ZEKE: Say, Slappy.

VERITY: Yes, Pappy?

ZEKE: What's a potato's least favorite day of the week?

VERITY: I don't know. What IS a potato's least favorite day of the week?

ZEKE: Fryday. Heh…heh…anyway.

VERITY: Heh…anyway…

ZEKE: Heh…

VERITY: Potato humor…

(Lights off of VERITY)

ZEKE: So, when our politics started to divide us we stopped performing together. We stopped laughing together. We suddenly couldn't agree about anything. And that was…sad. Things hit rock bottom when she volunteered for the Kruger campaign.

(VERITY *is carrying some signs.* "Unclog the Bog", "Burn
her up!", "Women are incapable of rational thought!", "God
hates Hags!" *etc.*)

ZEKE: What are you doing?

VERITY: I'm moved to political action for the first
time—

ZEKE: Why him?

VERITY: Zeke— Like he said— He's going to make the
colonies tolerable again—

ZEKE: —Oh, the colonies have always been tolerable—

VERITY: Please, if it wasn't for the astronomical infant
mortality rate this place would be hell on earth.

ZEKE: Well, yeah— But he's a liar, Verity! He'll tell you
anything you want to hear to get elected.

VERITY: What about Goody Bending? Huh? She doesn't
pander?

ZEKE: Absolutely not!

(Lights up on GOODY BENDING *giving a speech at a rally!)*

GOODY BENDING: A vote for me means a vote for
whatever ye want a vote for me to mean!

(Lights off of GOODY BENDING.*)*

ZEKE: That wasn't the strongest slogan…

VERITY: See!

ZEKE: But at least she's sane and competent!

VERITY: What about when it's that time of the month!?!

ZEKE: Then she's cranky, sane, and competent!

VERITY: What if she's bloated— You know what, I can't
have this argument with you right now, Zeke. I've got
to get to my charity work.

ZEKE: Making rally signs is not charity work.

VERITY: I'll have thee know I made these signs for a bunch of underprivileged white nationalists who I share absolutely nothing in common with except our political affiliation! Zeke, I'm standing up for what I believe in for the first time and you just can't stand me disagreeing with you! *(She storms out.)*

ZEKE: I'm—I'm storming out, too! *(He goes outside and sits.)* Damn it.

(Their goat, STANDISH walks up and nudges him.)

ZEKE: Oh, heya, Standish. You're a good goat. Maybe she's right. Maybe I am so interested in my side winning I'm acting as irrationally as I think she's acting? But I'll eat my hat if what she's fighting for aren't some patently bad ideas wrapped in a patently putrid package.

STANDISH: Maaahhhh.

ZEKE: Awwe…you love alliteration.

STANDISH: Maaahhh.

ZEKE: You just— You just think you know someone and then…I don't know…

STANDISH: Maahhh.

ZEKE: You won't vote for a fascist, will you?

STANDISH: Maaahhh.

ZEKE: No— No you won't. I love you. Yes, I do.

STANDISH: Maahhh.

ZEKE: These human problems don't touch you do they? Oh, to be more like you Standish. Just to be a good… no, a great goat.

STANDISH: Maaahh.

(STANDISH licks ZEKE's face all over. ZEKE half-heartedly tries to make him stop.)

ZEKE: Sto— Stop—Standish, now. Stop. C'mon...
Yucky! *(He keeps petting* STANDISH *while he speaks to us.)*

ZEKE: Things got way more dramatic on election night
after the town went insane and elected Kruger.

(Lights off of ZEKE *and* STANDISH *and up on three girls,*
TRINA, MARY, *and* DOTTY. DOTTY *is in bed, unconscious.*
MARY *and* TRINA *are tying to wake her.)*

MARY: Please wake up! How long has she been this
way?

TRINA: Since father caught us dancing in the woods!
She's putting on to avoid being punished. Wake up!

MARY: Dotty! Please! People are saying there is
witchcraft at work!

TRINA: People say that?

MARY: People say they saw Dotty flying over the
rooftops before landing in the woods with all of her life
drained from her by some hellish fiend.

TRINA: Oh, my god, people are so stupid.

MARY: I know but they believe it! And if they hear we
were dancing they'll think us witches!

TRINA: Dotty! Wake up!

MARY: Dotty!

TRINA: Dotty! We'll be hanged, the lot of us if ye do not
snap out of it!

MARY: Please Dotty! If we just admit to dancing we'll
be whipped and that's all! But if they think the Devil is
at work—

TRINA: Dotty, we know you're putting on! We know!
I swear to God, Dotty, if thou doesn't wake up at this
moment I will shit in thy mouth!

MARY: I've seen her do it!

TRINA: That's it—

(*She starts pulling up her dress and climbing on the bed.* DOTTY *wakes up!*)

DOTTY: Don't shit in my mouth, Trina!

(TRINA *grabs her.*)

TRINA: Aha!

DOTTY: Please, father will whip us raw if he knew we were looking to sign our names in Black Phillip's book! I was just dancing!

TRINA: We were all just dancing!

DOTTY: You drank blood! I saw you!

TRINA: It was just a little blood!

DOTTY: Ye sacrificed a goat and ate its heart while begging the devil to bugger thee to death!

TRINA: Oh, I barely did that.

MARY: It was sport, that's all!

TRINA: Right! A merry lark, with fire and blood—

MARY: —In an attempt to unlock the cage of hell—

TRINA: That's all!

(TRINA *and* DOTTY's *father,* JACOB HORNER, *enters.* DOTTY *collapses again.*)

HORNER: Has she stirred?

DOTTY: No!

HORNER: Damn it!

MARY: Mr Horner, the town is abuzz with talks of witchcraft!

HORNER: What?

MARY: They say Dotty was seen flying over the rooftops!

HORNER: Who is saying that?

MARY: All of the stupidest people in town!

HORNER: Ohmygodohmygod! They drive the public conversation! Leave us, Mary. I need to speak with my daughters. Say nothing to no one about anything ever!

MARY: Umm, okay. *(She exits.)*

TRINA: It was just sport, father! We were only dancing to the top ten at ten countdown!

HORNER: I swear to god, Trina, if thy delinquency here puts a stain on the good name of this righteous household I will shit in thy mouth.

(HORNER starts to take off his belt. DUNNING enters with his Chief of Staff, DEVIN HARRIS.)

DUNNING: I am here.

DEVIN: Excellent point, sir.

HORNER: Reverend Kruger! Congratulations on thy victory!

DUNNING: I couldn't have done it without thee and the other forty-six people who voted for me. Forty-seven out of a hundred. A resounding majority!

HORNER: To what do we owe the honor?

DUNNING: Everyone in town is saying thy daughter is very sexy.

DEVIN: Possessed. They're saying she's possessed.

DUNNING: Oh, possessed?

DEVIN: People are saying she's possessed by the Devil.

DUNNING: I heard sexy.

DEVIN: Possessed.

DUNNING: Then why are we here?

HORNER: My daughter, Dotty, has merely taken ill.

DUNNING: Let me see. Hmm, I think you're right, Devin. She's not sexy. What is she twelve?

HORNER: Yes, Reverend. And here is my other daughter, Trina.

DUNNING: Whoa, how old are you?

TRINA: Seventeen.

DUNNING: Play ball.

(VERITY *enters.*)

VERITY: Reverend Elect Kruger, all of the morons in town are saying the Devil is in this house!

DUNNING: Thank ye...

DEVIN: Goody Farmer.

DUNNING: —Goody Farmer but we already know that because I know exactly what every moron in town is thinking. Me not know why. Plus, me sense the Devil here!

(*There's a gasp.*)

VERITY: Oh no!

DUNNING: I'm really, really, really good at sensing the Devil. Maybe the best. I know pretty much everything about everything and have a perfect memory. Tell us, Mr...um...

DEVIN: —Horner—

DUNNING: Palmer. What happened?

HORNER: Well, about a fortnight ago—

(DEVIN *whispers to* DUNNING.)

DEVIN: —Two weeks—

DUNNING: —Ah!

HORNER: I was in the woods for my evening constitution and I heard music and followed the sound and discovered every young girl in the village dancing!

(Everyone gasps.)

HORNER: And they were totally naked.

(Another gasp.)

DUNNING: Nice.

HORNER: They were dancing naked around a boiling cauldron and my slave, Zwena, was stirring the cauldron and chanting in a foreign tongue.

VERITY: Oh, my goodness!

HORNER: And every night for the next two weeks, I would take my place behind a bush, and every night the girls would come and disrobe and gyrate—their young, pale bodies lit by the glow of the moon!

(There's another gasp.)

HORNER: Tonight I stepped on a branch and snapped a twig which alerted the girls to my presence. When they saw me they screamed and fled in every direction!

VERITY: So...let me get this straight. You hid behind a tree—

HORNER: —Yes—

VERITY: —And secretly watched all the young girls of the village dance...

HORNER: Uh, huh.

VERITY: ...naked...

HORNER: That's right.

VERITY: For two weeks.

HORNER: Yes.

VERITY: And you're just telling us this tonight, only because they caught you watching them?

HORNER: That sums it up neatly.

VERITY: And we're thinking the GIRLS have done something wrong?

HORNER: Yes.

DEVIN: Absolutely.

DUNNING: What's thy point, woman?

VERITY: Nothing, I guess.

DEVIN: What we need to do now is investigate.

DUNNING: Yes, I love investigating! I'm one of the all time great investigators. What do we do now?

DEVIN: We question the slave. Let the slave in.

DUNNING: Hey, I'm the boss. Let me say the stuff.

DEVIN: Of course, Reverend Kruger.

(Beat)

DUNNING: Let the slave in. Good? Was that good?

DEVIN: Wonderful, sir.

(HORNER's slave, ZWENA, enters.)

ZWENA: What the hell, people? Why're you calling me here? I'm on the brink of a great discovery.

HORNER: Zwena! Our new Reverend is here. Show some respect.

ZWENA: Oh, shit. My bad. What's up reverend dickhead?

HORNER: Zwena!

ZWENA: What? I didn't vote for this sack of shit.

HORNER: Zwena!

ZWENA: I didn't vote for anybody, did I? I'm not allowed to vote. I would have voted for the crone with the stiff-ass haircut though, not this crusty motherfucker.

HORNER: Zwena, hold thy tongue, woman!

DUNNING: We have questions for you, slave. First of all, what do you mean crusty?

ZWENA: Ye look crusty as hell. You're old and thy body looks like a bag of boogers and you might be the dumbest person any of us have ever met.

DUNNING: Well...you're a loser.

ZWENA: Nice insult, ya homeschooled toilet wand.

DUNNING: ...L-Loser...

ZWENA: What do ye want? It's got to be quick. I think I've discovered tiny living organisms, smaller than the eye can see, that make us sick! I call it my 'Germ theory of disease'.

DUNNING: Do you know how crazy you sound?!

DEVIN: What kind of witch talk is this?!

HORNER: Apologies, Reverend. In her homeland she was a witch doctor.

ZWENA: A witch doct—? Man, I was pediatrician!

DUNNING: Aha! And THAT ladies and gentlemen is why we can't allow more immigrants into this country! Let them have their way and we'll be overrun with "pediatricians"!

(The rest of the room applauds DUNNING. He loves it.)

ZWENA: What. The. Hell?

HORNER: Immigrants are ruining this country!

ZWENA: You literally kidnapped me and brought me here. Shit.

HORNER: Listen to me, slave. Tell us what was happening in the woods tonight?

ZWENA: Ohhh—in the woods?

HORNER: The woods. Tell us.

ZWENA: Nothing.

HORNER: I witnessed devilry and debauchery! I witnessed chanting and naked dancing and a bubbling cauldron. When the girls noticed me they ran as only the guilty run! I pulled up my pants and gave chase—

VERITY: Why were you—

HORNER: What?

VERITY: I'm sorry, why were your pants down?

HORNER: Me thinks that's beside the point.

DUNNING: It's beside the point, woman.

VERITY: Well, it seems like maybe a new point—

HORNER: Will ye let me—

DEVIN: —Let him finish his story, woman!

DUNNING: Know thy place, woman!

HORNER: Know thy place—

VERITY: I ju—

DUNNING: —Thy place is not to question why a good Christian man has his pants around his ankles in the middle of the woods while—

VERITY: —But—

DUNNING: —WHILE he watches young girls frolic in the nude—

DEVIN: Know thy place—

HORNER: Know it—

DUNNING: Right, so just…just shut the fuck up and listen to his story for a second! Go ahead, Horner.

HORNER: Thank ye. I was…I can't remember where I was—

DUNNING: You were putting your wiener away.

HORNER: Right—

VERITY: —Jesus Christ.

HORNER: And I chased the screaming maids until I found my daughter enchanted by a devil you invited into the town, slave!

DUNNING: Confess, slave!

ZWENA: Damn! I know I'm a slave ye don't have to keep calling me that!

DEVIN: We know ye were leading these girls in witchcraft. Confess!

HORNER: What of the bubbling cauldron?

ZWENA: I was boiling the town's drinking water so half of ya'll don't die from Cholera again!

DUNNING: Cholera?! How stupid do thee think we are?

ZWENA: Very fucking stupid.

DUNNING: Confess and ye will be hanged! Deny it and ye will be burned!

ZWENA: Oh, hell no! I want more choices!

HORNER: Listen, you evil slave—

ZWENA: Oh, I'm your slave and I'M the evil one. Okay. Okay. How about this? Thy little white girls wanted me to call up Black Phillip so they could sign up in his devil book and I'm like, "Oh, ye think I'm gonna know him just because he's black? Like we all know each other?" So, I say, "Okay, I'll take thy skinny asses out in the woods and make ye dance around naked and catch pneumonia ya bunch of stuck up twats."

DUNNING: Watch thy language!

ZWENA: Oh, fuck thee!

DUNNING: You have to show me respect! If not me, then you must at least respect the sovereignty and dignity of the holy office that I hold! (*He rips an enormous fart and loves it.*) I gotta claim that one.

DEVIN: Good one, sir.

TRINA: I heard ye speaking the devil's language!

ZWENA: I was speaking French ye ignorant slit.

HORNER: Tell us the truth! Tell us ye called the devil and to whom else he speaks! If ye do we shall spare thy life.

ZWENA: You want me to snitch? Oh, I'll snitch. Who do ye want me to snitch on?

HORNER: What about John Prior? Does he speak to the Devil?

ZWENA: Ye know it.

(Everyone gasps.)

HORNER: He does?!

ZWENA: Oh, hell yeah. He talks to the Devil all the time.

HORNER: And Goody Tompkins. Does she talk to the Devil?

ZWENA: Talk to him? She's got the devil on speed dial.

DOTTY: *(Rising)* I saw the Devil! I saw the Devil in Peabody!!

HORNER: Dotty!

VERITY: She wakes!

DOTTY: I saw the Devil! I saw Goody Tomkins with the Devil! I saw Goody Wright with the Devil!

TRINA: Yeah, that's the ticket…I saw Goody Wright with the Devil! I saw J J Barea with the Devil! I saw Luca Doncic with the Devil!

DEVIN: Those are my teammates!

DOTTY: I saw Devin Harris with the Devil!

DEVIN: Me??!

DUNNING: Hey, that's my chief of staff!

TRINA: I saw Dunning Kruger with the Devil!

DOTTY: I saw Dunning Kruger with the Devil!

DUNNING: Hey!

VERITY: They're just accusing the last person that spoke!

(Beat)

TRINA: I saw Goody Farmer with the Devil!

DOTTY: I saw Goody Farmer with the Devil!

VERITY: No you didn't!

TRINA: We did! We did see them with the Devil!

DOTTY: We did! We did see them with the Devil!

TRINA: Dunning Kruger and his campaign colluded with the Devil to sway the election in his favor!

HORNER: You deny this?

DUNNING: Yes!

VERITY: Absolutely!

TRINA: They're witches!

DOTTY: WITCHES! WITCHES! WITCHES!!

TRINA: WITCHES! WITCHES! WITCHES!!

ZWENA: *(Aside)* This country is fucked.

HORNER: You know what this means!? We have ourselves a crucible!

(Gasp!)

VERITY: Another one?! Awe, man.

(Black out. Lights up on VERITY in a cell. ZEKE enters, carrying flowers. He's led in by CHEECH, a guard.)

CHEECH: Visitor.

VERITY: Oh, Zeke!

ZEKE: Hey, sweetie.

VERITY: Zeke, you came.

ZEKE: Of course, I came. *(To* CHEECH*)* You mind if we have a little privacy?

CHEECH: Five Minute. *(He leaves.)*

ZEKE: Five minute. Singular. You know his name is Cheech? Cheech. He's gotta be the first Cheech, right?

VERITY: Oh, Zeke, you brought me flowers.

ZEKE: Yeah, I thought it was the least I could do.

VERITY: They're beautiful.

ZEKE: You hanging in there?

VERITY: It's terrible.

ZEKE: What happened?

VERITY: I was with Reverend Kruger and Devin Harris at the home of Markus Horner and his two daughters—

ZEKE: All the girls were dancing naked in the woods.

VERITY: How did you know that?

ZEKE: Hm? Oh… No reason… The rest, however, is a mystery.

VERITY: Well, then Mr. Horner's slave started accusing people of witchcraft and then his daughters joined in and named the Reverend, Devin, myself and the rest of his campaign.

ZEKE: That's terrible.

VERITY: The flowers are beautiful.

ZEKE: Read the card.

VERITY: Awwe… *(She reads.)* "I told thee so." Zeke!

ZEKE: I told you not to associate with those men!

VERITY: Honey, don't rub it in, please. I just—I just liked how hard he promised to be on China. This is just a witch hunt!

ZEKE: Well...

VERITY: What? You don't think I—

ZEKE: —No— Of course, not. But sometimes when you go on a witch hunt you find witches—

VERITY: I—you know I know that—

ZEKE: I know—

VERITY: I was way out in front of the—

ZEKE: —The sexual harassment—

VERITY: —I coined the term for the "And I, As Well Movement."

ZEKE: Right.

VERITY: And that wasn't a witch hunt—

ZEKE: That's what I'm saying. You're not a witch but that doesn't mean he isn't—

VERITY: —Damnit, let's—

ZEKE: —Sorry—

VERITY: —Let's not argue more about—

ZEKE: —I'm sorry. I just knew that it would turn out like this.

VERITY: They're going to burn me alive, Zeke!

ZEKE: I thought that was best case scenario. But they're not burning my wife. Check the flowers again.

(VERITY *pulls out a saw.*)

VERITY: Zeke!

ZEKE: Shh!

(VERITY *pulls out another saw. And another. And another. And another*)

ZEKE: I thought you might need options. Nice— Nice nature scene painted on this one...

VERITY: Pretty, where'd you get that?

ZEKE: Cracker Barrel.

VERITY: Hm.

ZEKE: Okay. I'll call Cheech back in here and you pretend like you're sick. While he's checking on you, I'll choke him out, then we'll shag ass.

(ZWENA *speaks up from the darkness.*)

ZWENA: That's not gonna work.

ZEKE: Why not?

ZWENA: Cheech is a beast and you got way too much sugar in thy shorts.

ZEKE: They're not shorts. They're pantaloons.

VERITY: What's your plan?

ZEKE: —Everybody wears them—

ZWENA: My plan? I plan on being burned at the stake.

VERITY: I thought they were gonna spare you.

ZWENA: Yeah, they're gonna spare the sister. Sure. Sure.

ZEKE: Well, we gotta try something.

VERITY: Okay. Go for it.

ZEKE: Ready?

VERITY: Ready.

ZEKE: I love you.

VERITY: I love you, too.

ZEKE: Even though you are sooo stupid for vot—

VERITY: Zeke!

ZEKE: Okay.

ZWENA: He's not wrong.

ZEKE: Cheech! Cheech!

(CHEECH *enters.*)

CHEECH: What is it?

ZEKE: I think she's sick.

VERITY: Oh, I'm bad! It's real bad. Cough, cough.

CHEECH: What wrong?

VERITY: I think I have… hepatitis C…

CHEECH: What?

VERITY: No— My—my bosom. It's a problem with my bosom. They won't stop heaving. Will you take a look?

CHEECH: Oh, no. Not you bosom. I look.

(CHEECH *goes to check* VERITY's *bosom.* ZEKE *tries to climb up* CHEECH *to get his arms around his throat in several different ways but* CHEECH *is too big and* ZEKE *doesn't know the first thing about it.* VERITY *vamps a little.*)

VERITY: When I inhale they go way out like this, etc.

ZWENA: You're doing great.

ZEKE: He's not even noticing.

ZWENA: I told ye, bro. We're gonna die.

VERITY: Hurry! This scene is getting problematic!

ZEKE: *(Aside)* So, I wrestled with Cheech for a while. He thought it was fun.

CHEECH: That tickle!

ZEKE: You're an animal, Cheech! Jesus, you're cuddly. I love it.

(CHEECH, ZWENA, *and* VERITY *are gone.*)

ZEKE: Anyway, then the trial started.

(A light rises on JUDGE STURM, *looking stern. Court music underscores.)*

ZEKE: The honorable Judge Sturm was presiding. A man wound so tight he had his own daughter declared a witch and put to death for inventing cornflakes.

JUDGE STURM: It was a flake most unnatural.

ZEKE: Took another two hundred years before someone else got the idea. Heh... Anyway... The trial was a fiasco! The accused lost their lawyer almost immediately.

(Lights up on the court)

JUDGE STURM: Let it be known that this trial shall be fair and balanced. This court will be very careful not to allow this witch hunt to become a...witch hunt. Now... let the accusers speak and let us believe them no matter what they say!

DEFENSE ATTORNEY: Umm... Objection, your honor.

JUDGE STURM: The defense has an objection? On what grounds?

DEFENSE ATTORNEY: On what gr— I—I object to the fact that ye open the trial by saying the accusers will be believed no matter what...

TRINA: Witch! Witch!

JUDGE STURM: Get this witch out of my court!!!

DEFENSE ATTORNEY: Ah! Jesus!

(The DEFENSE ATTORNEY *is whisked away! The* PROSECUTOR *steps forward. Like any good lawyer, he has a deep south drawl.)*

PROSECUTOR: Your honor, we'd like to call Trina Horner to the stand.

TRINA: Witch!

PROSECUTOR: What?

TRINA: Sorry. Habit.

PROSECUTOR: Trina. Is it true that thou has't accused several people in this room of witchcraft?

TRINA: Yes, I have.

PROSECUTOR: Your honor, I rest my case.

(The court erupts.)

JUDGE STURM: Order! Order in my court!

(The court comes to order.)

JUDGE STURM: Order I say! I will have order! Order! Order in this court! There. It seems the prosecution has rested and the defense has been himself accused of witchery so I find the—

ZEKE: Wait! Wait a second!

JUDGE STURM: What's this!?

ZEKE: I have a few questions, if I may?

JUDGE STURM: This is—sir, a lawyer ye be?

ZEKE: No. A lawyer not I be. I'm a farmer. But nobody's a lawyer here. This guy's not a lawyer. What do you do?

PROSECUTOR: I am into leather.

ZEKE: He— I— Sorry? You're…

PROSECUTOR: Into leather. Privately, I wear leather… breeches, vests, collars, chaps, little cute—cute little hats…and I meet up with others who, like me, are also wearing leather.

ZEKE: Like, assless pants?

PROSECUTOR: Right.

ZEKE: Okay—I get it.

PROSECUTOR: There's a little group of us.

ZEKE: So, you just hang out?

PROSECUTOR: More or less.

ZEKE: Huh—

PROSECUTOR: —We also rail each other.

ZEKE: —There it is. Right. And, Your Honor, do you yourself have a law degree?

JUDGE STURM: I do not.

ZEKE: And what qualifies you to preside here?

JUDGE STURM: I…was not busy.

ZEKE: You weren't busy?

JUDGE STURM: I—I don't have any friends anymore.

ZEKE: And why is that?

JUDGE STURM: They say I'm too—I'm too judgey. So…

ZEKE: Okay— Trina— Can I call you Trina?

TRINA: My name is Trina.

ZEKE: Trina, did you really see all of these people talking to the Devil?

TRINA: Yes.

ZEKE: Really?

TRINA: Yes.

ZEKE: I mean, like, really really?

TRINA: Yes, really.

ZEKE: God, I am not good at this.

VERITY: You're doing great!

TRINA: I saw them all dancing with the devil.

ZEKE: Aha! Was it hilarious?

TRINA: What?

ZEKE: Was it hilarious when you saw them dancing with the Devil?

TRINA: No, why it was terrifying!

ZEKE: Well then you couldn't have seen my wife dancing because it is always hilarious!

VERITY: I thought I was a sexy dancer.

ZEKE: Oh, honey, you are a sexy dancer if you're attracted to someone flopping around like they have a head injury...and I am! I am! Show them—show the court.

PROSECUTOR: Objection your honor!

JUDGE STURM: I'll allow it. Dance, woman.

VERITY: Okay...

(VERITY *dances. The court provides a beat. She starts hesitantly but then gets a little confidence and gets into it. Then, abruptly—)*

JUDGE STURM: Let the record show that Verity Farmer dances like an insane person.

PROSECUTOR: I withdraw my objection, your honor. She moves like a bird that has been struck by a large rock.

VERITY: I hate everybody!

TRINA: Ezekiel Farmer, we have, all of us, countless times, heard ye tell anyone who would listen that thy wife was a witch!

(There's a general consensus.)

ZEKE: A—a bitch. I said she was a bitch. Heh... Is it true, Trina, that the only reason you've accused my wife is that you're in love with me?

(Pause)

TRINA: Damn, thee! I love thee with all of my heart, Ezekiel Farmer!

ZEKE: I did— That was a real shot in the dark.

TRINA: I have loved thee from the moment we met.

ZEKE: Really?!

TRINA: I was churning butter and you were watching me churn butter. Remember?

ZEKE: There have been so many—

TRINA: But thy wife is a witch! I'll never recant!

ZEKE: No further question—

TRINA: Ezekiel!

ZEKE: You are dismissed!

TRINA: I LOVE THEE!!

(ZEKE *has to dodge* TRINA.)

ZEKE: Ah! (*To us*) Devin Harris's time on the stand was certainly instructive.

(*The lights shift to* DEVIN *on the stand.*)

DEVIN: My name is Devin Harris. I am a humble public servant. My aim is to ignore the dangers posed by an oafish dullard who I understand is absolutely an existential threat to the planet merely in order to achieve legislative measures that are designed to siphon money from the working class in order to enrich myself and my wealthy, shadowy benefactors, the Koch Brothers. But I am no witch.

ZEKE: I think, your honor, that we'd all like to kick this man square in the nuts—

(*There's a general consensus.*)

ZEKE: But that doesn't make him a witch! It makes him selfish and cynical and just a real piece of crap.

(*More agreement. To us:*)

ZEKE: By the time I had Kruger on the stand I was fully in lawyer mode. (*He speaks with a Georgia accent.*) Reverend Kruger, can I call you that?

DUNNING: That is my name.

ZEKE: Reverend Kruger, you love the Bible?

DUNNING: I do. I love it so, so much. It's maybe the—it is THE greatest book ever written.

ZEKE: And what is your favorite book in the Bible?

DUNNING: That is a trick question. The Bible is a book therefore it does not contain other books. It has pages.

ZEKE: Uh, huh. What then is yo favorite verse in the Bible?

DUNNING: All of them. My answer is all of them. That's a perfect answer.

ZEKE: Uh...HUH. What's this?

DUNNING: I know that by a mere glance, mind ye, to be the good and Holy Bible or our God.

ZEKE: Ohhhh! Ye know it's da Bible?!?!

DUNNING: I do.

ZEKE: Okay/ Could you read this verse here for me? The one underlined?

DUNNING: This one?

ZEKE: Yes.

(Beat)

DUNNING: The words with the line drawn under them?

ZEKE: Just read it.

DUNNING: Heh...I don't have my spectac—

ZEKE: Here they are.

(ZEKE hands DUNNING some glasses.)

DUNNING: Heh... thanks. Thank ye. Ahem. D... D... O... O... Doh— DOH! Doh! Doh uh...uh...nn...Doh unn...t, t...t...o...o.... Doh— Sorry. Doh untoe—

(To us:)

ZEKE: Literally forty five minutes later—

DUNNING: Doh untoe aht-hers ass yo-uh woe-uld hahvee t-heem doh untoe yo-uh. *(He tosses the Bible away.)* There! I passed thy fucking reading test! I can read.

ZEKE: Sure you can. Now what does it mean?

DUNNING: It means go to Hell and shut up!

ZEKE: So, you are the new Reverend of Peabody?

DUNNING: People said I couldn't win and I won! Eat my balls, haters!

ZEKE: Why do you think they thought you couldn't win?

DUNNING: Did you just hear my last sentence?

ZEKE: Right. Why did you run for Reverend?

DUNNING: I love the guy up there in the sky place. The guy with the beard. And the—locusts and whatnot.

ZEKE: God?

DUNNING: Yeah. Him. Love him. Terrific guy. Terrific. A pretty shitty Dad but nobody's perfect. And— Look, I wanted all of the people who didn't like me to have to sup upon my butthole for at least four years!

PROSECUTOR: I object, your honor! These questions are merely designed to show that his client is wildly incompetent and disgusting.

JUDGE STURM: I must say it's working…

PROSECUTOR: Your honor, being a heavy, sweaty, odd looking sociopath with a skid mark for a personality and colon polyps that look like Portobella mushrooms doesn't make a person a witch!

(REVEREND HALE enters in a panic.)

REVEREND HALE: STOP THE TRIAL!

JUDGE STURM: Reverend Hale!?

REVEREND HALE: Pray, tell. Am I in time? Is anyone condemned a witch?

JUDGE STURM: My sentence is forthcoming—

REVEREND HALE: Oh, the lord is good. I have come from Salem where thy Brothers and Sisters in Christ have wrongfully sentenced nineteen innocent men, women, and children to death. I tried to stop them. Lord help me, I tried, but their vitriol was so potent, their disdain for reason so profound, that I fear my pleas for justice could only fall on willfully closed ears. Please, I beseech thee, Peabody, reject the madness of Salem. Look on the faces of thy neighbors. They are no devils. They are mere mortals, guilty of sin, aye. But let those of us not guilty of some earthly transgressions rise now that we may see thy spotless hide...I thought not. Please. I understand that this man, thy new Reverend here—

(REVEREND HALE *puts his hand on* DUNNING's *shoulder.* DUNNING *pats his hand.*)

DUNNING: Yes.

REVEREND HALE: I know that he, frankly, is the walking distillation of ignorance—

DUNNING: Hey—

REVEREND HALE: —and a phantasmagoria of nasty behaviors. I know he represents all that is wrong and vile and petulant about our culture—

ZWENA: Preach!

REVEREND HALE: I suspect he's some kind of Evil Chauncey Gardiner... But let us not stoop. No. Let us not forgo our reliance on the observable fact merely to settle some score. Let us not revel in the incrimination of another. For if we do then we are no better than this rank, immoral, childish, butterball turkey in men's clothing. This is no way to resist this man. Ladies and gentlemen, brothers and sisters, the road to Hell is paved not with good intentions. It is paved with lies.

(Pause)

TRINA: Witch! Witch!

JUDGE STURM: No! Now! Shut up, you! Reverend, Hale, thy council is well reasoned and thy reputation proceeds thee. And frankly, I find the way thy mouth moves more than a little mesmerizing.

REVEREND HALE: Thank ye.

JUDGE STURM: I fear this court has acted in haste.

TRINA: No!

JUDGE STURM: Seeing demons where there are merely men, however loutish, bigotted, and offensively stupid they may be…I…I find all defendants innocent of the crime of witchcraft!

(The court erupts with shouts and celebration.)

ZEKE: We did it!

VERITY: Honey!

(TRINA approaches VERITY and ZEKE.)

TRINA: I'll not forget how ye embarrassed me here.

ZEKE: Great. See that you don't.

TRINA: You'll pay—

VERITY: Screw off, ya fuckin' hole. I'm celebrating with my husband.

(VERITY and ZEKE kiss.)

ZEKE: You called her a hole.

VERITY: I know!

ZEKE: That's so cool.

(The court has cleared of all but them, DUNNING, DEVIN and the PROSECUTOR.)

DUNNING: Everyone! Fellow defendants come here, I'd like to say something to thee. I know this has been a terrible few days for all of us. And I'd like to thank ye for sticking with me here even when things weren't looking so good.

DEVIN: Our pleasure, sir.

VERITY: I'm just happy we're all safe.

DUNNING: Yeah, yeah... And also—

(His voice changes to that of an amplified, hellish fiend. The lights change.)

DUNNING: THANK YOU, SATAN!

OTHERS: THANK YOU, SATAN! HAIL SATAN!

(They all hail Satan and laugh demonically.)

DUNNING: AFTER MY INAUGURATION, WHICH I EXPECT WILL BE HUGE, THIS TOWN WILL BE BATHED IN THE BLOOD OF THE INNOCENT!! THE GENTLE SHALL FEAR US! THE RIGHTEOUS SHALL QUAKE BEFORE US! PERSONAL TRAINERS WILL HATE US FOR THIS ONE WEIRD TRICK TO KILL BELLY FAT!

(They laugh demonically. VERITY side steps out of the group to ZEKE.)

VERITY: We gotta go—

ZEKE: What is it?

VERITY: Witches. Witches! They're real witches—

ZEKE: Wha—

VERITY: They're really real—

(VERITY and ZEKE are gone. Leaving only the others still laughing demonically. The laugh peters out. They all still speak with a amplified, demon voices, though casually.)

DEVIN: I don't know about anyone else, but I am starving.

DUNNING: Famished!

(They're all hungry. The lights are fading.)

DEVIN: Where should we go?

DUNNING: Cyndi's Deli?

DEVIN: I could nosh.

(Black out)

END OF ACT ONE

ACT TWO

(Lights up on ZEKE in his cell)

ZEKE: Welcome back, God. I hope you had a great intermission. Refilled thy widdle sippy cup. I mean, you're the creator of the universe, you'd think they'd trust you with a little wine in a shitty old theater. Jesus. Anyway, where were we? Ah. Dunning Kruger was a witch. His whole posse was a bunch of witches. A lot of people knew.

(A PURITAN couple strolls by.)

PURITAN MAN #2: He's a witch!

PURITAN WOMAN #3: I KNOW!

PURITAN MAN #2: It's TERRIBLE!

PURITAN WOMAN #3: I KNOW!

PURITAN MAN #2: HE'S RUINING EVERYTHING!

PURITAN WOMAN #3: I KNOW!!

PURITAN MAN #2: THIS IS THE SCARIEST TIME TO BE ALIVE!

PURITAN WOMAN #3: I KNOW!!

(Beat)

PURITAN MAN #2: Where does't thou want to eat lunch?

PURITAN WOMAN #3: Cromwell's?

PURITAN MAN #2: We had Cromwell's on Tuesday.

PURITAN WOMAN #3: Wait, it's a little early for lunch.

PURITAN MAN #2: Even better. Brunch!

PURITAN WOMAN #3: What the fuck is brunch?

(They're gone.)

ZEKE: Some people loved the new normal.

(Another couple strolls by carrying muskets.)

PURITAN MAN #3: Finally, got our town back.

PURITAN WOMAN #4: Peabody is our town and it's back
to the way it used to be. I feel safe again.

PURITAN MAN #3: I've never felt safer.

*(Something startles them and they point their muskets at
EVERYTHING.)*

PURITAN MAN #3: What—

PURITAN WOMAN #4: Did thou—

PURITAN MAN #3: Shh...

PURITAN WOMAN #4: What sound did thou hear?

PURITAN MAN #3: Methought I heard...the rustling of
leaves...

*(Pause. They shoot their muskets at EVERYTHING. They
slowly make their way off stage, shooting the whole time.)*

(Lights up on the DENTIST *looking at* TRINA's *teeth.)*

DENTIST: Hast thou been praying for thy teeth after
every meal?

TRINA: Thou knows I've not.

DENTIST: Hmm... Yes, it is just dreadful in here. *(He
goes about his work.)* What does't thou make of our
reverend?

TRINA: Hm? Oh, passing tolerable... You?

DENTIST: Well... sure... passing tolerable... I mean,
does thou think he colludes with the devil?

TRINA: Probably. But whatst canst thou do?

DENTIST: Exactly, whatst canst thou do? That's exactly what Ezekiel Farmer was saying—

TRINA: EZEKIEL FARMER!? EZEKIEL FARMER!?!?

DENTIST: Uh, huh. That guy's nuts.

TRINA: Nuts? How do ye mean, nuts?

DENTIST: Obsessed with butter churning he is.

TRINA: Yes?

DENTIST: Yah! Obsessed?! Ezekiel farmer is a sick puppy—but thou didn't hear it from me.

TRINA: Sick puppy, eh? Obsessed, eh? Excellent...

DENTIST: Okay/ I'd like to try some experimental dentistry. I'm going to try hitting thy teeth with this hammer.

(Lights down on DENTIST and TRINA.)

(Lights up on VERITY and ZEKE eating dinner in silence for a bit.)

ZEKE: Good.

VERITY: Mm. Thank you.

ZEKE: The salad—

VERITY: I grilled it.

ZEKE: Grilled it?

VERITY: I know. Who grills salad? But it totally works.

ZEKE: Yeah.

VERITY: You can taste the smoke in there.

ZEKE: I tasted smoke.

(Pause. VERITY starts to cry. ZEKE, to us.)

ZEKE: She's been doing this for the last year... She hasn't forgiven herself for helping Kruger into office.

VERITY: Today…he appointed the village idiot to be the new school marm!

ZEKE: Betsy!?

VERITY: Betsy! Teaching!

ZEKE: Betsy was simultaneously kicked in both sides of her head by two different horses!

VERITY: I know!

ZEKE: She's a vegetable!

VERITY: And now she's teaching the next generation and that's my fault!

ZEKE: Kids are dumb enough as it is!

VERITY: She'll just teach them to mumble and collect string!

(VERITY *cries again.* ZEKE, *to us:*)

ZEKE: The most frightening thing this last year is reading the Peabody Press— (*He holds up a handwritten and hand drawn newsletter.*) Every day it's a new horrifying story. Verity, listen to this. It says here, "Ahhh! Ahh! What?!?!? Oh, God! Oh, God! Ahhh!!" Man, things are bad.

VERITY: I j— I just can't take it anymore! Between this and bankrupting us with his lavish parties and vacations, picking fights with every other village, the fucking Indian wall, and pressing all the journalists to death with large stones…I—I— We have to do something!

ZEKE: Do something? Wh— Like what!?

VERITY: Like…surround ourselves with like minded people.

(*Suddenly, with some fun effect,* VERITY *and* ZEKE *are in a meeting of like minded people who're all sitting in a crisscross applesauce in a semicircle. TESSA is speaking.*)

TESSA: Verity and Ezekiel Farmer are joining us today. Welcome friends.

ALL: Welcome, friends.

TESSA: Come, have a seat in our bubble. Here. Make thyself comfortable and be not afraid to speak thy mind. This is a safe space.

ALL: Safe Space.

VERITY: W— Well, all right.

TESSA: You'll find this is a welcoming, inclusive, nonjudgemental environment.

ALL: Inclusive. Nonjudgemental.

ZEKE: How do they know what to repeat?

(VERITY *hits* ZEKE.)

VERITY: Thank you for having us.

TESSA: All are welcome.

ZEKE: Welcoooo— Sorry, I guessed wrong.

TESSA: Have a seat with us.

VERITY: Okay—

ZEKE: You—ah—you have a chair?

TESSA: Ezekiel, I'll remind you gently to check your privilege.

ZEKE: My—

MARVIN: There are people in this world who haven't any furniture.

TESSA: They've been forced by centuries of systemic pressures to forgo those items you take for granted—

MARVIN: —Furniture—

SANDY: —Clean water—

DIRK: —Healthy food—

TESSA: —Access to affordable health care. Tell me when your humors are tinged with yellow and you've been prescribed a round of leeches what doest thou do?

ZEKE: I pop down to the local hideous swamp hag and pick up some leeches—

TESSA: —Oh, Ezekiel, thy privilege is, frankly, stultifying.

MARVIN: —Check your privilege—

DIRK: —Check it—

ZEKE: —It— It's checked— I—I'm sorry I didn't know—

TESSA: You didn't know?!

MARVIN: Of course, you didn't—

DIRK: WE forgo those luxuries—

ZEKE: You don't own furniture?

TESSA: Of course, we own furniture—

DIRK: —Sleek—

MARVIN: —Comfortable furniture—

SANDY: —Of Scandinavian design!

TESSA: BUT WE PREFER NOT TO TALK ABOUT IT HERE IN OUR INCLUSIVE, SOCIALLY CONSCIOUS CHAT ROOM!

ALL: SOCIALLY CONSCIOUS CHAT ROOM!

ZEKE: Right—sorry. I think we just got off on the wrong—uh—I'm just like thee. I swear. I spend like eighty percent of my day letting everybody know how woke I am.

ALL: Woke.

ZEKE: Right. Yeah— Sorry—it's just my back.

SANDY: Oh! People long to have backs!

DIRK: What about the backless!?

TESSA: YES, OH, I'M SO SORRY YOUR POOR WIDDLE WHITE MALE BACK HURTS.

DIRK: FUCKING WHITE MALE—

ZEKE: You're a white ma—

VERITY: Honey, sit your—your white back down— It's not that bad... Here. These are our people. We share their values. We're for equal treatment of all men and women no matter their background, race, economic standing or creed. We all see the dangers before us and we are the reasonable ones. All we have to do is work together and we can change this new reality.

TESSA: Hear this woman speak the words that will nourish and heal this land. Hear this woman. This goddess. Verily, we say...

ALL: Yaaaaaaassssss.

(ZEKE starts to sit uncomfortably.)

VERITY: Yaass. Yas.

ZEKE: Yep. Yas. I'm in.

VERITY: Right. Just— Honey, just sit Indian style—

ALL: WHAAAA!?!?!?!?!?!?!?!? INDIAN STYLE?!?!?!?

(They meld into a many headed serpent.)

ALL: DIE BITCH WHORE!!!!! SSSS!!!!

VERITY: AHHH!!!! SHIT!

ZEKE: Run!

(VERITY amd ZEKE scream and dodge until they've left the serpent behind. They take a moment to catch their breath.)

ZEKE: They were nice—

VERITY: You just HAD to have a chair!

ZEKE: I'm forty!!

VERITY: Well, exercise every now and then—

ZEKE: I—

VERITY: —Some strength trainin—

ZEKE: I don't LIKE WEIGHTS!

VERITY: You're skinny fat!

(ZEKE *gasps!*)

VERITY: Oh... Oh, I'm sorry.

ZEKE: It's okay—

VERITY: No—

ZEKE: No, it's fine.

VERITY: Honey...I've always loved thy Farmer Bod. You know that—

ZEKE: ...They called me a white male.

VERITY: You are a white male.

ZEKE: Yeah, but they don't have to call me that! A few centuries of raping the planet and genocide and brutal subjugation of other cultures and building country after country on the bones of the people who were there first and suddenly we're the bad guys?

VERITY: Well, yeah—

ZEKE: Shoot. I—I think this is giving me all the feels.

VERITY: I'm so sorry— This— It's making us all fight amongst ourselves.

ZEKE: I know. I liked the safe space people a lot until they...fucking turned into a serpent and tried to kill us.

VERITY: It's just— It's up to us.

ZEKE: Us? Me and you?

VERITY: Zeke, we are morally obligated to resist this man.

ZEKE: We can't do—

VERITY: Of course, we can!

ZEKE: Well…

VERITY: I mean, we know—we KNOW that he is in league with the devil.

ZEKE: Right—

VERITY: He's not just a buffoon with bad hair. He's evil, Zeke. We have to stop him…

ZEKE: Stop… Stop him—how are— Look, what can we do to resist someone so powerful?

VERITY: We tell everybody he's a witch.

ZEKE: That's played out.

VERITY: Okay… Then we're going to… We're going to have to break into one of his parties and prove to everyone he really is a witch. Get him to witch out.

ZEKE: Witch out?

VERITY: Yeah.

ZEKE: That's a great plan. Look, honey, two normal nobodies like us can't do anything. The best we can do is lay low and wait him out. None of these changes have really…affected us that much, you know?

VERITY: Have you read page two of the paper?

ZEKE: What? There's a page 2? *(He flips the paper over to the other side.)* Oh—what's this goat thing—

(Lights up on the other side of the stage. DUNNING is giving a speech.)

DUNNING: Okay— The goat plan— The goat plan. Ye like the goat plan? People who don't have very many goats, okay, those people will give their goats to the people who already have a lot of goats. So— So, all the goats will be owned by just a few people—

(A voice heckles him.)

HECKLER: Boo!

DUNNING: Now—now—

HECKLER: What about me?! I ain't haveth no goat!

DUNNING: Somebody get that sonofabitch outta here!

(The crowd cheers.)

DUNNING: Get him out! Out! I'd like to punch that guy in the face!

(The crowd loves it.)

DUNNING: In my day—the late 1500s—we'd torture that guy's butthole with all kinds of crazy stuff!

(The crowd loves it.)

DUNNING: Yeah! Sharp stuff! Hot stuff! Rats! Whatever! That's what I'd like to do to that guy!

(Cheer)

DUNNING: Anyhoo. Where was I? The goat plan! The goat plan. And the goats will love this plan. They'll be all pinned in together, hot, sweaty, with nothing to do but plow each other. That'll lead to more goats. And all the rich awesome people will run outta room for these goats. See? So what you'll get—what the poor, dirty people will eventually get is trickle down goats. See? The goats will trickle down...

(Lights off of DUNNING)

ZEKE: What the actual fuck?

VERITY: See?

(We hear STANDISH bleating from the yard.)

STANDISH: *(Off)* Maaahhh!!

ZEKE: Standish!

(VERITY and ZEKE rush into the yard. A FED is carrying STANDISH off.)

STANDISH: Maaahhh!

ZEKE: Put my goat down!

FED: In accordance with goat law this goat be the property of thy betters!

ZEKE: Standish!

STANDISH: Maahhh!!!

ZEKE: Standish!!

STANDISH: Maahhh!!

(STANDISH *and the* FED *are gone.*)

ZEKE: STANDISH!!!! STANDISH! SHIT, this is DRAMATIC!!! STANDISH!

(ZEKE *collapses.* VERITY *comforts him.*)

VERITY: We'll fight this. We'll get the best goat lawyer—

ZEKE: We can't—

VERITY: But—

ZEKE: We can't afford a goat lawyer!

VERITY: Zeke—

ZEKE: No!... No... First—first they came for the chickens... And I did not speak out.

VERITY: Honey—

ZEKE: Because I had no chickens. Then they came for the cows and I said nothing. Because I had no cow. Then they came for the goats.

VERITY: Oh, Zeke.

ZEKE: My body is ready. Let's do the expose him as a witch in front of the entire town thing.

VERITY: Yes!

ZEKE: *(To us)* But to do that, we'll need a plan...and a team.

(*Music plays. The next bit should approximate a movie montage where the leads put together a crack team for a heist. It could be filmed or done live…*)

ZEKE: We'll need some muscle.

(CHEECH *is in the middle of a bare knuckle prize fight against two guys. He knocks them both out.* ZEKE *steps from the shadows.*)

ZEKE: You just won me a lot of money big guy—

(CHEECH *turns and reflexively knocks* ZEKE *out.*)

CHEECH: Zeke! Cheech sorry!

(*Lights out on* CHEECH *and* ZEKE *and up on* VERITY.)

VERITY: We'll need someone inconspicuous on the inside…

(ZWENA *is stirring a witch's brew.* VERITY *steps from the shadows.*)

VERITY: Zwena, my old friend—

ZWENA: The fuck you want?!

VERITY: Oh— I just—

ZWENA: What?

VERITY: I—

ZWENA: What is it?

VERITY: Sorry—

ZWENA: Sorry what?

VERITY: Ah—

ZWENA: Shit, spit it out, woman.

VERITY: Okay— We need—

ZWENA: I'm in.

(*Lights off of* VERITY *and* ZWENA *and back on* ZEKE)

ZEKE: Boom! We had our mouth and our muscle, our brain—

VERITY: Who's the brain?

ZEKE: Hm—oh, I'm—

VERITY: —You?

ZEKE: What?!

VERITY: No, fine—

ZEKE: What?

VERITY: No, you're the brain—

ZEKE: —Well, it was—

VERITY: —Right—

ZEKE: It was my idea—

VERITY: —Yes, you're the brain, honey. You're the brain.

ZEKE: Okay— We had the Mouth, the Muscle, the brain, and the beauty.

VERITY: Awwee!

ZEKE: See, I'm the brain but that's because you were going to be the beauty—

VERITY: That's good.

ZEKE: Yeah?

VERITY: I'll take it— Though I'm part brains—

ZEKE: That goes without saying.

VERITY: That's sweet.

ZEKE: How about you're the Beauty who also has brains?

VERITY: That's good.

ZEKE: Yeah?

VERITY: Yeah—

ZEKE: K... Little long but—

VERITY: Okay—

ZEKE: We had the Mouth, and the Muscle, the Brains, and the Beauty who also has brains. Now the only thing we need?

VERITY: The Bitch.

ZEKE: The Bitch.

(*Blackout. Lights up on a dark, spooky wood.* ZEKE *and* VERITY *enter.*)

ZEKE: These woods are creepy-A-F.

VERITY: Are you sure this is where she's hiding?

ZEKE: Yeah. She's been spotted wandering these woods since election night. God, I hate nature.

VERITY: I know. I look forward to a future where everything is paved.

ZEKE: Amen—

VOICE: Whoooo...

ZEKE: What was that!?

VOICE: Whooo—

VERITY: —It's an owl—

VOICE: Comes into mine wood unbidden?

VERITY: It is Verity and Ezekiel Farmer.

VOICE: Begone ye farmers! There be no life in these soils. There be only fear. There be only pain. Regrets be all doth be growin' in these wood.

ZEKE: Goody— Goody Bending? Is that you?

(GOODY BENDING, *hooded and bent, steps into the light.*)

GOODY BENDING: Aye!

(VERITY *and* ZEKE *scream!*)

GOODY BENDING: I be what be left o' the one afore be called Goody Bending.

(GOODY BENDING *removes her hood with a sting of music. She's very menacing. A witch of the wood*)

ZEKE: God. You look like shit.

VERITY: —Zeke—

ZEKE: —This year has not been kind to you—

GOODY BENDING: I be hauntin' this wood—I be a ghost—a ghost still be breathin'.

ZEKE: So, you haven't been brushing your hair at all?

(GOODY BENDING *hisses and circles* VERITY *and* ZEKE.)

VERITY: Zeke— Good morrow, Goody Bending. We came looking for you.

GOODY BENDING: Then ye be lookin' wrong ye be! *(She laughs.)*

ZEKE: Well, she's a whacko—

VERITY: Goody Bending, we—we've come for thy help.

GOODY BENDING: Me help. Me help! Ha! Goody Bending be no help—no help Goody Bending be.

VERITY: We offer you redemption.

GOODY BENDING: Ha! Redemption! They be offerin' redemption. No redemption in hell there be.

ZEKE: She talks like a really stupid pirate—

VERITY: Shh—

GOODY BENDING: A question she be havin' for ye.

VERITY: Yes?

GOODY BENDING: Did ye be votin'… Votin' for Goody Bending? Eh? Did ye?

ZEKE: I did! Twice. Heh. Kidding. Once. I voted for you.

GOODY BENDING: Ye be liberal?

ZEKE: Oh—yeah. Very liberal. Very empathetic and progressive and totally and stridently intolerant of non liberal view points.

GOODY BENDING: Good! As god intended. And ye??

VERITY: Hm? What was the question?

GOODY BENDING: Ye stink of bad ideas—

VERITY: He was going to Unclog the Bog—

GOODY BENDING: Unclog the Bog! Unclog the Bog!

VERITY: It rhymed—

GOODY BENDING: Oh, it rhymed!!

VERITY: And I agreed, generally with the sentiment!!! You're all hot, hot garbage! The whole fucking system. The back stabbing and the two faced word salad—I wanted to do my part to break the whole thing. To burn it to the ground. I voted with my middle finger. Look, he appealed to my worst self and now my worst self is running things. Taking people's chickens, and cows—

ZEKE: And goats.

GOODY BENDING: Goats!? He be selling trickle down goats to ye?

VERITY: Yeah, trickle down goats.

GOODY BENDING: Aye… Aye. It's always been about the goats. There alway been two sides in the great battle there be.

ZEKE: Good and Evil—

GOODY BENDING: —Nay. They who be fer trickle down goats…and they who be fer trickle up goats.

ZEKE: Aha.

GOODY BENDING: Eider way—the goats is gonna end up at the top!

(GOODY BENDING *laughs crazily. After a beat* ZEKE *laughs with her then, while still laughing.*)

ZEKE: You're a lunatic!

VERITY: Help us! Help us destroy him, oh insane one. For he's a witch who consorts with the devil and though that's kinda cool—

ZEKE: —It's super cool—

VERITY: —If he was in a band—

ZEKE: —Right, different story then—

VERITY: Right— But he shouldn't be in charge of innocent people's lives.

(*Pause. Music builds.*)

GOODY BENDING: Goody Bending, she be walkin' the wood, bidin' her time, growin' her bush to monsterous proportions…just waitin' for a chance to be shoving a big one up Dunning Kruger's stinky turd cutter, she has… It's her help ye be gettin'!

VERITY: Yes!

ZEKE: Our team is complete!

(*They all high five and freeze mid-high five for a few moments. Finally, they release it.*)

VERITY: Soo…

GOODY BENDING: …Ah! Here. The weapon ye be needin'. (*She pulls out a jar of liquid and removes the lid.*)

ZEKE: Weapon?

GOODY BENDING: Me creation— (*She sniffs it deeply.*)

GOODY BENDING: Holy fire.

VERITY: Holy fire?

GOODY BENDING: Douse the devil witch and set ablaze he be. The magic mask be burned away—

VERITY: And we'll see the witch beneath!

GOODY BENDING: Aye.

(GOODY BENDING sniffs it again and hands it to VERITY.)

VERITY: What is it?

GOODY BENDING: Accelerant. Refined petroleum—

VERITY: Oh. Gas, right? *(She sniffs it.)* Whoa!

(VERITY sniffs it again. ZEKE grabs it.)

VERITY: Oh, my god.

ZEKE: Lemme see— *(He sniffs it.)* Strong stuff.

(ZEKE takes a deep inhale or two. VERITY takes it and huffs it.)

VERITY: Woo!

(GOODY BENDING takes a huff. VERITY grabs it and takes two big huffs.)

VERITY: Oh, shit.

(GOODY BENDING takes a huff. ZEKE reaches for it.)

ZEKE: Here— Ye be passin' that ye be—

VERITY: Me turn ye be skippin'?

(They argue as GOODY BENDING laughs like an old hag.)

(Blackout. Lights up on the crew. ZEKE, VERITY, ZWENA, and CHEECH. They're bent over a map, actively pointing, planning for a bit. Have fun. ZEKE looks up and speaks to us.)

ZEKE: We stayed in the woods with Goody Bending for what felt like hours and—and it turned out to be weeks. We got deep—

VERITY: —DEEP—

ZEKE: —DEEP into the Holy Fire scene. It was not pretty—

VERITY: —We woke up two weeks later in Georgia covered in tasteless tatoos.

ZEKE: Right. But we eventually got our shit together, dried out a little, and started planning.

VERITY: Cheech, you use your new position as Kruger's body guard to stay close to him.

CHEECH: Stay close.

ZEKE: You'll stand guard outside his room to make sure no one comes in while we're in there. Got it?

CHEECH: Cheech, got.

ZEKE: Thank you for coming over to our side.

CHEECH: Cheech no be a party to endless, bald-faced mendacity no more.

ZEKE: God, you're a dream to work with. I love you.

CHEECH: Cheech love Zeke, too.

ZEKE: Zwena, have you figured out how you're getting into the party?

ZWENA: Yeah, I got a job with the catering company.

VERITY: Really?

ZWENA: Yeah.

VERITY: A job?

ZWENA: A job. I'm a caterer.

VERITY: Are they paying you?

ZWENA: Man, fuck you.

ZEKE: O— Okay— Caterer is good. It's perfect. You can sneak the Holy Fire into the party with the food and drink.

ZWENA: Got it.

ZEKE: Now this is important. You are not to give the Holy Fire to either Verity or myself until RIGHT before it's going to be used—

VERITY: No matter how much we beg ye for it—

ZEKE: —And we WILL beg ye for it—

VERITY: Beg. Plead. We'll scream. We'll threaten ye—

ZEKE: —We'll lie—

VERITY: —We're gonna git up in yo shit about it—

ZEKE: —We'll offer sexual favors for it—

VERITY: —Super sick stuff.

ZEKE: Whatever you're into—we'll do it, man—

VERITY: —Yeah, REALLY sick stuff. C'mon, just say the word—

ZEKE: What's the word—

VERITY: —Butt stuff?

ZWENA: I don—

ZEKE: —Is it butt stuff—

VERITY: —You can pee on us—

ZWENA: —I don't want butt stuff—

ZEKE: You wanna spank us? Huh?

ZWENA: Ya'll are unsanitary—

VERITY: —You like that? Lil' spanky spanky—

ZWENA: I don't want to spank ya'll! What the hell is wrong with you people?

VERITY: Sorry!

ZEKE: Just don't—

VERITY: —Don't let us near the Holy Fire.

ZWENA: Okay! Shit.

VERITY: Don't—

ZWENA: I won't! How are ya'll going to get ya'lls fucking FREAK ASSES into the party?

(Beat. VERITY *taps out a quick beat on the table, then:)*

VERITY: I'm Slappy!

ZEKE: And I'm Pappy!

VERITY: And we're the FARCEMERS!

ZEKE: And we're the FARCEMERS! Heh... FARCEmers...

VERITY: Say, Pappy!

ZEKE: Yeah, Slappy!

VERITY: What do Rednecks do for Thanksgiving?

ZEKE: I don't know! What DO Rednecks do for Thanksgiving??

VERITY: Pump Kin... Heh.

ZEKE: Pump. Kin.

VERITY: Heh, see...

ZEKE: Incest... Heh—

VERITY: Incest joke...

ZEKE: Heh...classy...

VERITY: Heh... Anyway...

ZEKE: Anyway...

ZWENA: *(To* CHEECH*)* As a product of incest, does that joke offend you?

CHEECH: Lil' bit.

ZEKE: It's—sorry—

VERITY: It's our act!

ZEKE: We're the entertainment!

ZWENA: They let you be the entertainment?

ZEKE: We auditioned.

VERITY: Since music has been outlawed—

ZEKE: —We're Puritans. We ran away from the Renaissance—

VERITY: —ALL art has been outlawed and they said what we do isn't considered art—

ZEKE: —Just a—

VERITY: —Just a series of vulgarities—

ZEKE: —So, we got the gig!

VERITY: I'm psyched!

ZEKE: Me too.

VERITY: Back on the horse.

ZWENA: You guys suck.

VERITY: Oh, we know.

ZEKE: Yeah, we're bad— So, the plan… After our set— Verity lures Kruger back to the greenroom by seducing him with her womanly wiles.

(VERITY *bites her lip and undulates her upper body.*)

VERITY: Uh. Uh.

ZWENA: Okay…

ZEKE: Verity, what you'll need to watch out for when you're in there alone is that he's a well known, serial masturbator.

VERITY: Yee—

ZEKE: Really. Don't ever accept a bowl of cereal from him.

VERITY: …um—

ZEKE: When the moment is perfect, yell out the code word…

VERITY: Razzmatazz.

ZEKE: Then, Zwena, I'll tweet you to let you know it's time—

ZWENA: What do you mean, you'll tweet me?

(ZEKE *whistles.*)

ZEKE: Then you retweet me—

(ZWENA *whistles.*)

ZEKE: Right. Then you give me the Holy Fire. Cheech lets me in the room and I douse him. He runs out, then I set him ablaze in front of everyone. His mask will be burned away and it will reveal the witch beneath.

ZWENA: So, we're burning him to death?

VERITY: No. The Holy Fire will just remove his human facade.

ZWENA: Ah…

VERITY: It's magic.

ZEKE: Goody Bending gave it to us.

ZWENA: Aha…

ZEKE: What?

ZWENA: Nothing. Hey, I'm good either way.

(Beat)

VERITY: Well… Okay.

ZEKE: Okay—

CHEECH: Okay—

ZWENA: Okay—

ZEKE: We have a plan… Can I get the Holy Fire—

ZWENA: Hell no.

(Lights down except a spot on ZEKE.)

ZEKE: We were ready—

(We hear a siren's song…the lights slowly rise on TRINA *churning butter.)*

TRINA:
Up and down
The Cream it rises
I will not stop
Up and down…

ZEKE: Watcha doin…

TRINA: Me?

ZEKE: Umm…yeah.

TRINA: Oh, my…I seem to be churning butter…

ZEKE: Oh, boy…

TRINA: Forget this path you're on…come with me…

ZEKE: Listen, I—I can't—

TRINA: ZEKE! …Thou are not a political man…

ZEKE: But Verity…

TRINA: She's a fool…forget her…when I'm done here thee will need a shitload of toast…

ZEKE: She needs me-—

TRINA: What can ye do? There be no fight in ye… just watch me turn this cream into rich velvety butter…

ZEKE: I…I… BEGONE YE DEVIL AND TAKE THY GOLDEN SPREAD WITH THEE TO HELL!

TRINA: EEEKKKK!!!

*(*ZEKE's *banished* TRINA.*)*

ZEKE: That was a close one… Anyway… The night of the party, everything was set and Verity and I were about to go on—

(Lights on VERITY *and* ZEKE *backstage)*

ZEKE: Who are we following again?

VERITY: Meatloaf.

ZEKE: Gross.

VERITY: I know.

ZEKE: He's been around forever.

VERITY: I know.

ZEKE: Hey...I'm sorry I was so hard on you before the election—

VERITY: No. I clearly made a mistake, and I, I mean I have to own it.

ZEKE: Well, I wouldn't have blamed thee if ye'd doubled down. I was a condescending jerk.

VERITY: ...Yeah...

ZEKE: I just was so flabbergasted by him I turned off my filter...

VERITY: ...Yeah...

ZEKE: And I'm glad you talked me into resisting. I was content to make fun of his terrible appearance, sink into a nearly equal and opposing cognitive dissonance, label everyone who disagreed with me a racist, and leave it at that.

VERITY: ...Yeah... Meatloaf is almost done.

ZEKE: Honey, I don't know what's going to happen today... So, I just want to you know that I love you.

VERITY: I love you, too. If we survive this...maybe it will bring us closer together.

They kiss.

ZEKE: Well, Meatloaf is done.

(Blackout)

VOICEOVER: Ladies and Gentlemen, welcome to the stage. Slappy and Pappy, the Farcemers!

(Lights up. VERITY *and* ZEKE *enter. We see* DUNNING *and* DEVIN *in a box together, watching the show.* CHEECH *is guarding them.)*

ZEKE: It's—uh, great to be here and following Meatloaf.

VERITY: I usually follow Meatloaf with a huuuge bowel movement...

(Beat. Hesitant rim shot)

VERITY: Heh...anyway...

ZEKE: Heh...vulgarity...anyway...

(The volume goes down on VERITY *and* ZEKE *and up on* DUNNING *and* DEVIN *as* ZWENA *comes by with a food cart.)*

ZWENA: HOT DAWWGS! HOT DAWWGS!!!

DUNNING: Woman!

ZWENA: What'dya want?

DUNNING: Fourteen hot dogs and four large sodas. Ya'll want anything?

(Lights back up on the performance.)

VERITY: Well, if April showers bring May flowers, what do Mayflowers bring?

ZEKE: Racists?

VERITY: No. Well, yes, but not what I was thinking—

ZEKE: Cult Members?

VERITY: Heh... Let's skip that one...

ZEKE: Umm... Well, Slappy, it's a shame that Plymouth Rock has been gentrified.

VERITY: Right. Shame. I mean it's cute.

ZEKE: Super cute.

VERITY: Lots of great new restaurants.

ZEKE: Plymouth Rock Roasters—

VERITY: Great coffee—

ZEKE: —GREAT coffee. Still, shame how the Natives build up a neighborhood—

VERITY: —Make it a cool neighborhood then here comes some Pilgrims and their coffee—

ZEKE: —and the Natives can't afford to live there anymore because, because they're dead...

VERITY: Right. Still...

ZEKE: Great coffee—

VERITY: —GREAT coffee... Ahem...

ZEKE: Heh...social satire...

(Exit music plays.)

ZEKE: That's it for us!

VERITY: You've been a great audience!

(VERITY and ZEKE "exit".)

ZEKE: Whew! We did it!

VERITY: Yeah! We didn't get a single laugh—

ZEKE: —It was like a waking nightmare—

VERITY: But we did it!

ZEKE: Yay! Hey— Dunning is looking this way...

VERITY: Ah... Time to turn it on. *(She walks her sexy walk towards DUNNING and DEVIN.)*

VERITY: ...Hey.

DUNNING: Hey.

VERITY: Ye may remember me from the show I just did.

DUNNING: Good show.

VERITY: Yeah?

DUNNING: It wasn't funny at all.

DEVIN: I didn't laugh once.

DUNNING: But then, I don't have a sense of humor.

DEVIN: Me either.

VERITY: Right... Right. If I couldn't make ye laugh...ye think I could make thee...moan...

DEVIN: —Yuuuuck.

DUNNING: —Niiice.

DUNNING: Devin, leave us.

DEVIN: Gladly. *(He exits.)*

DUNNING: I'm not really into Farmers.

VERITY: Why not?

DUNNING: They smell like dung.

VERITY: But you smell like dung.

DUNNING: Touche.

VERITY: And anyway, I'm not really a farmer—

DUNNING: No?

VERITY: That's—that's just my cover...

DUNNING: Cover? If thou aren't a farmer then what art thou?

VERITY: I'm...a...Russian hooker.

DUNNING: Ahhh... This news has opened my final chakra!

VERITY: I don't know what that means—

DUNNING: It means— Let's go make love...or as they say in Russia "Let's go pee on a bed."

(DUNNING's led VERITY to his room where CHEECH stands guard.)

DUNNING: After thee...

(VERITY enters the room and DUNNING hangs back. He puts his hat buckle on the door knob and winks at CHEECH.)

(He shuts the door.)

DUNNING: Would m'lady like a bowl of cereal? *(He produces a bowl of cereal.)*

VERITY: Gag— No— No thank—y—gag—you...

DUNNING: Suit thyself. *(He starts eating it.)*

VERITY: Razzmatazz!

DUNNING: Mm— Razzmatazz.

VERITY: Razz— RAZZMATAZZ!!!

DUNNING: RAZZMATAZZ!!! RAZZMATAZZ!!!

(ZEKE runs up to the door with the Holy Fire. He takes a huge huff of it for courage and bursts into the room.)

DUNNING: What art thou doing in here?!

ZEKE: We're with the resistance!

DUNNING: Protect me!

VERITY: I'm with the resistance, too.

DUNNING: I was going to pay for thy breast enhancement!

VERITY: Your reign has come to an end.

DUNNING: What fate doth thou see for me?

VERITY: We're going to douse ye with Holy Fire—

DUNNING: Holy Fire?!

ZEKE: And then we're going to show the world the face you're hiding beneath the face that is—is already pretty obviously ugly.

VERITY: You'll be subjected to a scrutiny you've never known.

DUNNING: I can't stand up to scrutiny! I'm like the embodiment of a million roaches. Shine light on me and I scatter in every direction! You're got me insulting myself!!!

ZEKE: Break yoself!

(ZEKE *charges* DUNNING *who ducks him and exits.* VERITY *and* ZEKE *follow. They chase him to the stage and chase him in circles.*)

DUNNING: Ladies and Gentlemen! Help thy reverend! Ah!

(DUNNING *slips by* ZEKE. DEVIN *appears and grabs* VERITY.)

DEVIN: I got her, sir!

DUNNING: Stop!!

(*Everyone stops.*)

DUNNING: Or my Chief of Staff and best friend in the whole world, Devin Harris, will break thy wife's neck.

VERITY: Do it! Zeke! Do it!

ZEKE: But thy neck!

VERITY: This is bigger than me. Look! All of these people are watching. They can see without a shadow of a doubt who he is. Do. It.

ZEKE: Honey…I love you… My… Us… In spite of our differences.

DUNNING: Awwe. Isn't that sweet?

DEVIN: It truly is.

DUNNING: I was being facetious.

DEVIN: I was…not sir. I— The way we treat each other matters… And I don't want to win at all costs.

DUNNING: What are ye talking about?

DEVIN: This…

(DEVIN *lets* VERITY *go.*)

DEVIN: This is not me. We don't have to be like this.

(ZWENA *sneaks up behind* DEVIN.)

DEVIN: I'm truly sorry for my complicity—

(ZWENA *cuts* DEVIN's *throat.*)

VERITY: Oh, shit!

ZWENA: We're playing hard ball now!

ZEKE: Zwena, he was on our side!

ZWENA: Ah… My bad.

VERITY: Zeke…douse him!

(ZEKE *starts to douse* DUNNING *and everything freezes. The lights shift abruptly to a harsh spot on* ZEKE.)

WOMAN'S VOICE: *(quietly calling:)* Zeke…Zeke…

(*On the other side of the stage,* TRINA *is revealed. She's churning butter.*)

TRINA:
Up and down
The cream it rises—

ZEKE: Do not tempt me woman!

TRINA: Come with me and forget thy troubles… Two more years is all that remains…

(VERITY *appears behind* TRINA *and kicks her between the legs.*)

TRINA: Ah—shit!

VERITY: Do it, Zeke.

(*The lights restore.* ZEKE *douses* DUNNING *who wails and doubles over in pain. Smoke fills the stage.* DUNNING *turns to reveal his witch face.*)

DUNNING: Here's Johnny!!

(*Everyone screams.*)

ZWENA: I didn't think that guy could look worse!

DUNNING: Help me father! Help me!!

(The Mouth of Hell opens. As Satan appears we hear the wailing of the damned. Satan is slightly effeminate and Russian.)

SATAN: Hello dare, hi dare, whatdoye want?

DUNNING: Save me!

SATAN: Ah, the Dunning Kruger. Why should I save ye?

DUNNING: I—am I not thy humble servant?

SATAN: Da. But ye don't need me. Look at thy people... Tell me what ye see...

DUNNING: They... They're going about their business... Counting the moments until can get back to looking at their phones.

SATAN: Da. They knew all along who you were and they know they can live with it. Whatst canst thou do? The ones that hated ye will still hate ye and some will have fun doing it. Lots o' laughs. But the one's who love thee... Most of them will love thee...I think out of spite...I don't know. It's hard to tell.

DUNNING: And...will I be reelected?

SATAN: Nyet. Not even close. But then I didn't think it was going to happen the first time.

DUNNING: It seemed improbable.

SATAN: It did. It really did... Anyhoo...I'll see ye in Hell...

(More wailing. He disappears and the lights come back to normal.)

DUNNING: You guys...are Losers! All of ye. I'm the winner! Again! I'm such a winner.

VERITY: We lost. Again.

ZEKE: Yeah... What was this all about?

VERITY: I don't know...

ZEKE: Hey...I love you.

VERITY: I love you, too. I do. I really, really do.

ZEKE: It's been fun—

VERITY: Yeah—

ZEKE: Putting our differences aside...

VERITY: Doing something together again.

ZEKE: Yeah...

(VERITY *and* ZEKE *hug. We hear a bleating from off stage.*)

ZEKE: Is that?

(STANDISH *enters.*)

ZEKE: Standish!!

STANDISH: Mahhhh!!

(STANDISH *runs to* ZEKE. ZEKE *holds him.* VERITY *holds them both.*)

STANDISH: Maaahhhh!!

(*The lights go to a spot on* ZEKE. *He talks to us.*)

ZEKE: I wish it would have ended like this. (*He walks over to his cell.*) Zwena was sentenced to being pressed to death with large stones for killing Devin.

(*Lights on* ZWENA *being pressed to death.*)

ZWENA: Put these words on my gravestone—
there is no way Dunning Kruger...has a...formal education. And heat your milk to temperatures of about 63°Celsius and maintain it for 30 minutes or, alternatively, heat to a higher temperature, 72° Celsius and hold it for at least fifteen...seconds.

(ZWENA *dies. Lights out on her.*)

ZEKE: She was full of all kinds of crazy talk like that at the end. Cheech was pressed to death with large stones for conspiring with us.

(*Lights on* CHEECH *under the stones.*)

CHEECH: Oooouuuuch…

(*Lights off of* CHEECH.)

ZEKE: Sorry, buddy. Standish was pressed to death with large stones, too.

(*Lights on* STANDISH)

STANDISH: Maaaaahhh…

(*Lights off of* STANDISH)

ZEKE: Ah, Standish…didn't know what was happening. And then… And then…of course.

(*Lights up on* VERITY *being pressed to death.*)

VERITY: Owww…

ZEKE: Verity…was it worth it?

VERITY: Umm…fuck yeah.

(*Lights off of* VERITY.)

ZEKE: Well… God? It's now or never to step in and, you know…

(*Pause. A* JAILER *comes for* ZEKE.)

ZEKE: Well…there you have it, Lord. Thanks for nothing… We had a pretty good time, though. Didn't we?

(*A noose descends in front of* ZEKE. *He puts it around his neck and sings.*)

ZEKE:
I can't stop the flow of history
with this rope around my neck

(*Lights up on* VERITY *again being crushed.*)

VERITY:
I can't solve this awful mystery
with this rock upon my chest

VERITY & ZEKE: *(Together)*
But that's okay,
Cuz I'm with you
I may be afraid
But I've got you

(Beat. VERITY *and* ZEKE *reach for each other's hands but can't quite reach.)*

VERITY:
This rock is kinda killing me
It's liquified my spleen

ZEKE:
This rope is literally killing me
and my pants are full of pee
(and not in a funny way)

VERITY & ZEKE: *(Together)*
But that's okay, I'm with you
I may be in pain
But I have you

(Lights up on everyone dying in one way or another.)

ALL:
We're DYYYYYYYYING
We're DYYYYYYYYYYYYYYING
We're Die die die die die die die dying

But that's okay, we'll die with you
You're at our play
so we love you

Just love your brother
and he'll love you
Just help your sister
And she'll help you

La la la la, la la la
La la la la la
La la al *(sorry La, Everybody!)*

Sing-Along

La la la la, la la la
La la la la la
La la la la

We're DYYYYYYYYYING
We're DYYYYYYYYYYYYYYYYYING
We're Die die die die die die die dying

But that's okay, we have you
Just love your sister
and she'll love you

Yeah, that's okay, we have you
Just love your brother
and he'll love you

(Black out)

END OF PLAY